Inspired
by Gina

Believe in Impossible Dreams!

Gina

Inspired *by* Gina

Poems of
Triumphant Faith

Regina Marie Blaylock

TATE PUBLISHING
AND ENTERPRISES, LLC

Inspired by Gina
Copyright © 2012 by Regina Marie Blaylock. All rights reserved.

No part of this publication may be reproduced, stored in a retrieval system or transmitted in any way by any means, electronic, mechanical, photocopy, recording or otherwise without the prior permission of the author except as provided by USA copyright law.

The opinions expressed by the author are not necessarily those of Tate Publishing, LLC.

This book is designed to provide accurate and authoritative information with regard to the subject matter covered. This information is given with the understanding that neither the author nor Tate Publishing, LLC is engaged in rendering legal, professional advice. Since the details of your situation are fact dependent, you should additionally seek the services of a competent professional.

Published by Tate Publishing & Enterprises, LLC
127 E. Trade Center Terrace | Mustang, Oklahoma 73064 USA
1.888.361.9473 | www.tatepublishing.com

Tate Publishing is committed to excellence in the publishing industry. The company reflects the philosophy established by the founders, based on Psalm 68:11,
"The Lord gave the word and great was the company of those who published it."

Book design copyright © 2012 by Tate Publishing, LLC. All rights reserved.
Cover design by Blake Brasor
Interior design by April Marciszewski

Published in the United States of America

ISBN: 978-1-61862-309-6
1. Poetry / General
2. Religion / Christian Life / Inspirational
12.02.09

Dedication

I dedicate this collection
To God, who touched me
And guided me unscathed
Through a fiery furnace.
My cup runneth over!

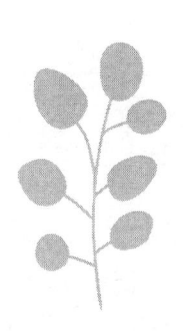

Introduction

Since I was a small child I've felt God's spiritual guidance. I am the middle child in a family of seven children. Raised in a Catholic family and brought up in Catholic schools, I've always had God in my life.

As I was just beginning my adult life, one of my brothers was diagnosed with schizophrenia. Then my eldest brother was diagnosed with cancer and died five years after he was diagnosed. A few years later another brother was diagnosed with schizophrenia. It was difficult to understand that two of my brothers had this diagnosis. The joy of motherhood touched my heart and I gave all to this. I love children and put my heart into my two children. Motherhood was comforting to me during this time. Soon my father, who I could tell my heart to, died. It was a time when I had to be strong to help my mom through this. But I felt alone because I realized he was the closest person to me.

I struggled forward, keeping all of my attention focused on my children. God began revealing to me that my life was not what I thought it was. My marriage ended and just as my life was beginning again, it took a sudden turn. My ex-husband committed suicide. Reactions from his death created even more turmoil and unrest in my life. People passed judgment on me because I filed for divorce. The person people saw was not the person we lived with. After his death, God revealed the lies, and I realized I never truly knew my husband.

In the midst of the storm, God caught me. He helped me find myself, my identity again, Gina. I became inspired. God protected me and my children from the storm around us. He renewed my life. He made me stronger and wiser. He taught me how beautiful and precious I am to him. The poetry rained down from him throughout my journey. Soon poems came to me in church and when others touched my life.

God gave me a beautiful home and friendly neighbors. I went on my first mission trip to rebuild Lakeshore, Mississippi, from hurricane Katrina. I went to give back and to help others find their home, but I gained so much more. God carried me and taught me the whole trip.

God is alive in my life. I know him like I have never known him before. He rains down beautiful blessings each day. My cup runneth over. I share these poems to inspire others to walk closer to him.

Table of Contents

	Poems of Faith	*11*
	Poems of Reassurance	*33*
	Poems of New Life	*49*
	Poems of Renewed Hope	*57*
	Poems of Fellowship	*65*
	Poems of Guidance	*71*
	Poems of Courage	*77*
	Poems of Love	*89*
	Poems of Eternal Life	*119*
	Poems of Grace	*125*

Poems *of* Faith

The following poems were written as I journeyed through difficult times. I wrote *Journey* when I went on a mission trip to rebuild Lakeshore, Mississippi with my church, The Journey. God nurtured and guided me on this trip and as I helped others rebuild their lives he was helping me move forward and rebuild my life. The poem *Journey* is dedicated to the pastor of my church.

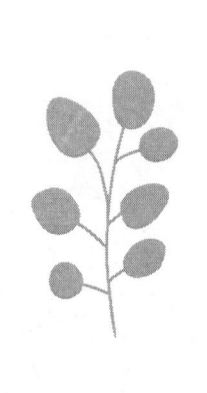

Journey

(Dedicated to Mike Harris)

Embarking on a path
With no road map

Following your heart
Wherever it may lead

Trusting in the unknown
The invisible winding path

Knowing not what is
Around the bend

Following the light
That beacon in the darkness

Spiritually filling your thirst
From streams of living water

Wrapping one another
With his eternal love

He leads us…HOME.

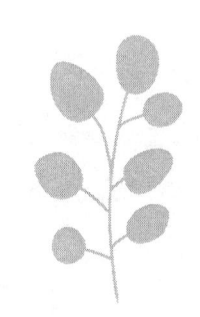

Wait on God

(Dedicated to Brian Dumas)

When times are troubled
Wait on God
When things are confusing
Wait on God
When there is nowhere to turn
Wait on God
When everything seems hopeless
Wait on God
To guide you
To lead you
Through the darkness
Into the light
Wait on God!

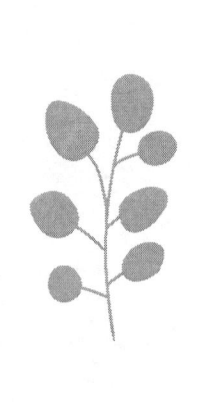

Details

God has given me a gift
A vision of my life
A new sight into the future
He does not tell me the details
But he shows me the results
He wants me to be happy
He knows what is deep within my heart
God sees me as a beautiful reflection of his love
He does not tell me the details

He asks me
To trust
To pray
To walk in faith
He promises me a future
Filled with endless joy
He does not tell me the details
He asks me to give a hundred fold
And my life will blossom
He blesses me…
Who needs details?

Worries

(Dedicated to Craig Collins)

When you can't sleep
And your heart is beating fast
Give your worries to God
When you are concerned
About what others say or think
Give your worries to God
When you can't make up your mind
When choices are difficult
Release the bindings from
Your heart and
Give your worries to God
For these burdens are
Too heavy for you to bear

God is here to release the weight
To lighten the load
So when pain is heavy
And your world seems very dark
Sit still—sit quiet
Listen
Give all your worries
To God!

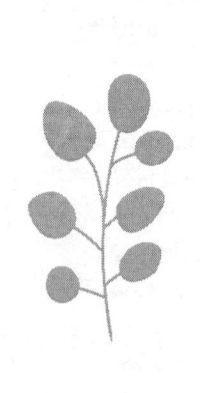

Walk By Faith

Today I walk by faith
For He walked with me
I want to despair
But He won't let me falter
I want to cry
But He holds me in His arms
I want to control things
But He shows me to release control
I have doubts
He reassures me with His promise
I am anxious
He settles me down
I am feeling distraught
He doesn't let me fall apart
He truly loves me
He truly wants everything for me

I walk by faith
Hand in hand
With He who
Tells me He loves me
He has forgiven me
I am His beautiful child
I feel warmth down
Deep inside
For Jesus walks holding my hand

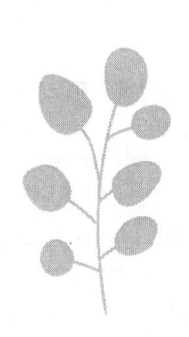

In the Palm of His Hand

God is holding me
In the Palm of His Hand
He is keeping me safe
Protecting me
He has a beautiful dream
Waiting for me
God is holding me
In the Palm of His Hand
Quieting my heart
Loving and caring for me
He knows I have been hurt
God is holding me
In the Palm of His Hand
He has healed me
Someone is coming my way
They are having a
Difficult time
God is holding me
In the Palm of His Hand
He is bringing
A new life
My way

Something beyond anything
I can imagine
God is holding me
In the Palm of His Hand
He has given me
Hope and Peace
God is holding me
In the Palm of His Hand
I wait patiently
For a new beginning
God is holding me
In the Palm of His Hand

Humility

Showing God through me
Joy in serving others
In His name
Not for glory
But for Love
God's Love to
Shine through me
To touch others
So they may open
Their hearts to God
Walking like Jesus
Seeing the beauty
That surrounds me
Listening in the silence
Walking with a
Peaceful heart
Not looking back
Following the journey
God has laid out for us
Offering a smile or hug
To lighten someone's
Load
Surrendering all to Him
Humility

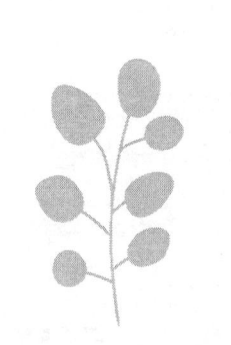

Steadfast

I will remain steadfast
In the light of the Lord
In His grace
His will be done
My light shines brightest
With Him
My love for Him is constant
For through Him all things come
My heart is with my Savior
Who loves and guides me
Deep within I feel
Great joy!

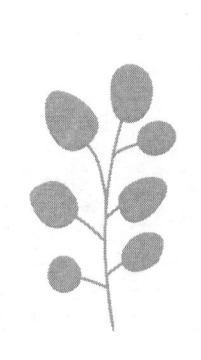

Angels

There are no angels
You say
But I know different
You've never seen them?
But I have seen them
They do God's work
They are His messengers
You don't believe in angels?
But I believe
They are something beyond
Explanation
Extraordinary, spiritual messengers
Of God
Ethereal in nature
You are moved when you see them
Breathtaking
There are angels
They come from God
They are His messengers
When you see them
You will never be the same
There is no question
There are angels

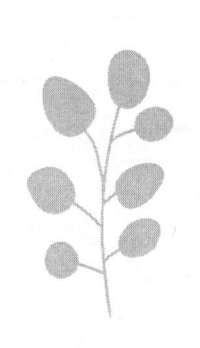

Tiny Lessons

Every day I learn tiny lessons
That shape and change
My life
God's grace is a gift
He gifts me because
He loves me
Give all your worries to God
Because we were not meant
To bear the burdens
That is why He came
Wait on God
Because He brings
Something more beautiful
Beyond your dreams
Protect your heart
Because that is where
The spirit of God lies

Live passionately
Because it gives
Your Life deeper meaning
Walk by Faith
Because God leads the way
In your life if you do
Drench your life with the
Spirit of God because its light

Shines through you
To show others the way
I am the way
The truth and
The light
Tiny lessons!

Poems *of* Reassurance

This collection of poems is written about God's reassurance that he is always with us, even in times when things are confusing. If we remain close to God, he can walk us through anything.

The poem *Heavenly Housing* is about a non-profit organization that was started after Hurricane Katrina by a passionate person from our church who just got in her car and went down to help.

Cleaning up the Mess is about my school district administration that did not keep the children as the center of their purpose. Because of this, many unworthy practices were taking place. Even in times like this, God is always there, and he can turn things around. He did just that in my school district. Sometimes God is right there under our nose and we fail to see him. People can see God in their lives when they look to the good things happening around them.

Peeling Away the Pain

God is peeling away the pain
Layer after layer
He removes the hurt
I have buried deep inside
Sometimes I awake
With my eyes full of tears
He reassures me
My fears are not reality
He removes the pain
And quiets my heart
I awake once more
With a heavy weight released
He has peeled back the pain
Taken hurts away
I am happier, calmer, more serene
I recognize His guidance
And purpose for my life
He keeps telling me to let go
Let Him lead me

It is easier
He wants me to be happy
Sometimes I am cautious
About a decision He wants me to make

He sends me angels
To reassure me I will be happy
I am learning trust and faith
In God's love
I have hope

Cleaning Up the Mess

God just opened the doors
And blew away the dust
Everything was wrong
Everything was upside down
But God walked in
Not a word did He say
He went straight to work
I watched in awe
At His Mighty Power
As He swept away
All of the dust and cobwebs
The deceit and manipulation
Everything shiny and bright
Then He went to work
On His people
Standing them upright
Helping them to walk
In the Light of His Love
In the silence
Not a word was spoken
He went to work
I watched in awe
God just opened the doors…
And blew away the dust!

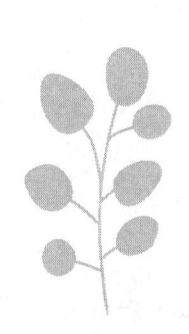

If You Could See Through a Child's Eyes

If you could see through
A child's eyes
What wonder and amazement
You would see
A world of possibilities
A world of beginnings
Everything fresh
Everything new
If you could see through
A child's eyes
Nothing could hurt you
There would be no pain
For the world is filled with
Excitement, adventures,
And change
If you could see through
A child's eyes
What love would surround you
All the beautiful things
God created
Would touch your
Heart!

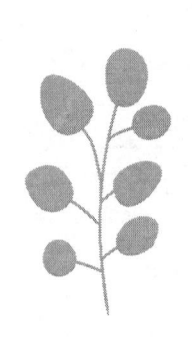

Cinderella Dreams

Cinderella dreams
Are about to come true
Lay aside your
Rags
Put on your
Beautiful gown
And glass slippers
For I am sending
You Cinderella dreams
That you could
Never imagine
You are beautiful
Inside and out
As you glow in your
Ball gown and
Dance with your
True love…
Prince Charming,
I shall shower
You with
My Love
And gifts of the Spirit
Cinderella Dreams
Are coming…soon!

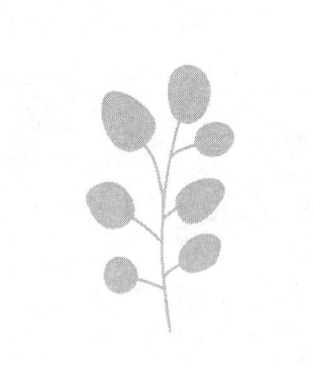

Heavenly Housing

(Dedicated to Lauren Brasile)

A haven of love
For a community
Of friends
Heavenly Housing
A sanctuary filled with
Hope
For those abandoned
And alone
Heavenly Housing
A place where
Faith, Hope, & Love
Reside
A rainbow of God's promise
To never forsake you
Heavenly Housing

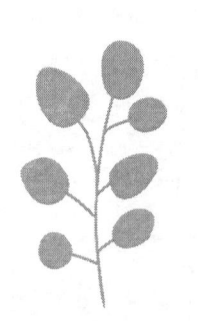

At the Dawn of the Day

At the dawn of the day
There are no worries
There are no fears
A beautiful sunrise
Begins the day
At the dawn of the day
Babies are waking up
To greet the day
A precious sight
For ours to see
At the dawn of the day
God's creatures
Are waking up
So many horizons ahead
At the dawn of the day
I pray
For God to bring
His promise
My way

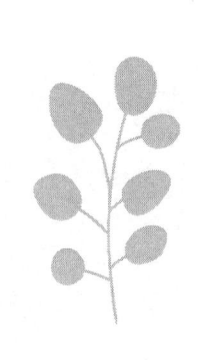

So Many Believe

So many believe
So few have seen
The miraculous works
Created by me
But I am here
Right here for all to see
The beautiful world
I have created for thee
So many believe
So few have seen
My mighty power
And the love
I shower
On those who seek me

So many believe
So few have seen
The grace and glory
Of me
But I am here
Right here
For all to see
Open up your heart
And follow me
And you will see
How glorious my works for you will be
And you will be blessed

Poems *of* New Life

These poems are about life and how God can give us new life. The poem *Reflections* is about how every life has a purpose and affects another life. Whether we realize it or not, we are all connected as one humanity under God.

Solmen's Place is a country estate owned by a family in our church. Every year our church does baptisms in the pond on this estate. It is a very beautiful expression of God's love to watch. I was baptized as a baby in the Catholic Church. When I returned from the mission trip in Lakeshore, Mississippi, I wanted to do a "believers" baptism there. It has deep meaning to me personally. It marked the beginning of a new life. I wrote *Wash It Away* after one of the baptisms.

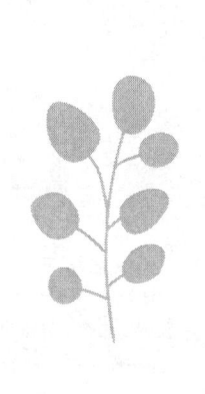

Reflections

An example of God's love in action
The turning of time
The memories of loved ones
The learning, growing, laughing together
A mirror of God's image
Displayed
Throughout your lifetime
The nurturing of generation after generation
The precious arrival of a new life
Reflections

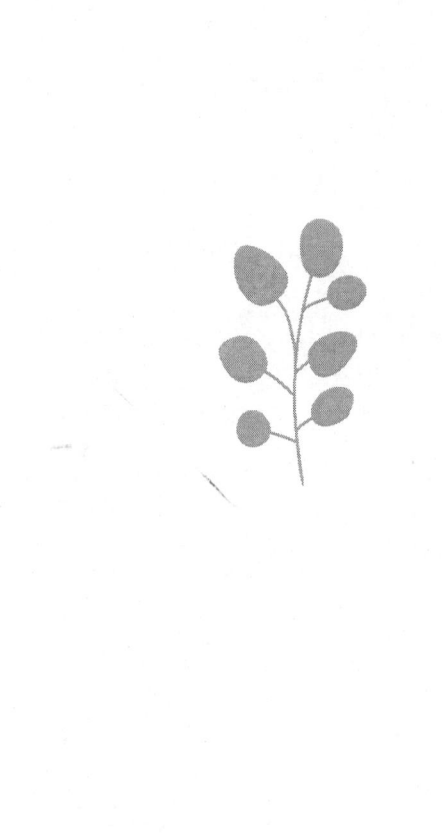

Solmen's Place

(Dedicated to Randy and Kim Solmen)

A Peaceful Sanctuary
Drenched in God's Love
Spiritual Healing
Encompasses Hearts
A Serene Pool
Of living waters
Amidst a country estate
A haven
Where God's Love Resides
And hearts
Soar in His
Image
Solmen's Place

Wash It Away

I ask God to wash away
The hurt and the pain
Wash away the
Worries and the sorrow
The rain comes pouring
Down on me
A gentle rain
A warm caressing rain
I ask God to wash
It all away
The grudges,
Fear, and anxiety
The rain comes harder
But it hits me
Gently
Washing away
All of the past

God washes it all away
He dries me in the
Warm sunlight of
His love
He shows me a
Rainbow and a future
Filled with
Happiness and love

Through Him
Today, God washes it all away
And
Wraps me in His
Love

Poems *of* Renewed Hope

When I arrived in Lakeshore, Mississippi, to help rebuild after Hurricane Katrina, it was very hot. I was thinking *What did I get myself into?* On the way down one of the leaders kept telling me he was going to show me how to build a deck. All I could think of was how hot it was and that I would never be able to handle that! Suddenly on the first job site someone asked, "Who wants to learn how to tile?" My hand was the first one up. We tiled two homes on that trip. I was fortunate to meet the owners and to hear their stories. As a part of the mission trip, we were to leave a life token behind. I wrote a poem on a tile for each home owner. The following poems are the life tokens I left behind. *The Tile Man* is dedicated to the man who taught me how to tile during the trip.

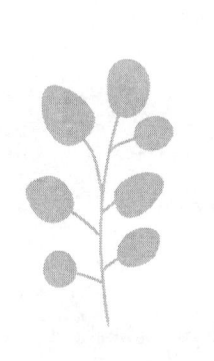

The Tile Man

(Dedicated to Steve Alvrez)

Piece by piece
Row by row
Patience, precision
An artistic masterpiece
Unfolds
No creation exactly
The same
Unique in ability and poise
Your life story
Laid out
Amongst many
Places

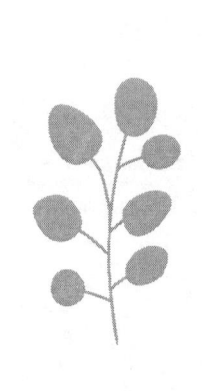

Warm Breezes

(Dedicated to Al and Bev Smith, Katrina Survivors)

Warm Breezes
Gently caressing our souls
Resting, Enjoying, Content
God's beauty before us
Fellowship, Lifetime friends
God Provides
He gives us all we need
He has extended your family
Throughout this country
Your story has touched
Many Hearts
And will go on
Beyond your years
The future displays
Only Rainbows

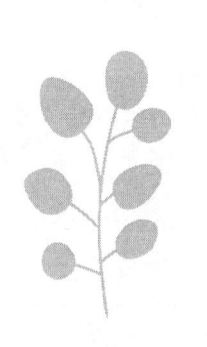

A Friendly Home

(Dedicated to the Cox family, Katrina Survivors)

No matter where you go
Or what you do
There is always a place
You can call home
It is not a building
It is not a collection of things
It is a place where
Warm memories have grown
Where familiar people and places
Hug your heart and soul
Remember
No matter how big or how small
You see the World
There is always a special place
Close to your heart
You can always call
Home!

Poems *of* Fellowship

These two poems are very special to me because they are about how important Christian fellowship is. The first one I wrote to a man at our church who saw my poems on tiles and felt they needed to be shared. He offered to help me launch my own website. This was a very difficult time for me because my ex-husband just committed suicide and putting my attention on my poems helped me through this. In return I passed on a monetary gift to our church. Some people from my church, including him, did not understand this at first. I wrote the poem to explain that when an act of kindness is done for us we are not indebted to that person but as Christians we pass a kindness on to others. Hebrews 13:16: "Do not forget to do good and to share, for with such things God is well pleased." If we give with our heart, we give openly and freely, not expecting anything in return.

The Bracelet was written after something spiritual happened in my small group amongst the women. When my ex-husband passed away, my life took an unexpected turn. I have two children, and I was the widow and in charge of all funeral and burial arrangements. A simple bracelet with crucifix charms was handed to me by my group leader to remind me that God was there, and he would get me through this. I wore the bracelet for a few weeks and then handed it to a woman in my group whose husband was having open heart surgery. Soon the bracelet was being handed around our group and other women in our church in times of crisis.

You Offered a Kindness

(Dedicated to John Gnotek)

You offered a kindness
A love for God
Nothing you asked in return
You just offered a
Kindness
Nothing would you gain
No judgment
Did you make
From your open heart
A deep understanding
Of God's Love
You offered a generous
Kindness
Overwhelming faith
You had in my
Talent
You took a chance
You offered an
Unforgettable kindness
I accepted
Your kindness
Offered during a dark time
Hope and belief
In a future

For my family
You offered a
Kindness
Never will I forget
Your kindness
In return
I passed on a
Kindness
To others
You just opened your
Heart
And offered a kindness
Never will I forget
Your kindness

The Bracelet

The Bracelet
A symbol of God's Love
In a circle of
Sisters in Christ
Passing from one Christian woman
To another
In times of spiritual challenge
To know that God is here
He is walking with us
Through difficult times
The Bracelet
Each charm represents
Christ's promise to never
Forsake us
He wraps His love
Around us and
Carries us on our journey
The Bracelet
Sisters in Christ
Walking with arms
Locked in His Love
The Bracelet

Poems *of* Guidance

These poems are about how in times of injustice God will reveal the truths and guide you through the darkness into his light.

God Bless Their Soul is a poem I wrote about how people treat one another based on what they see and hear but not necessarily on truths. Jesus said to speak only of good. Ephesians 4:29: "Do not let any unwholesome talk come out of your mouths, but only what is helpful for building others up according to their needs, that it may benefit those who listen." He is the only judge.

God Reveals Truths was written because in the confusion of my personal and professional life I would pray for God to help me discern the truths from the lies. He taught me how to be quiet and observe all that was around me. One by one he revealed the truths, some heart-wrenching and some that blind-sided me. But now God has my blindside. I can walk and trust only in him for he truly loves me and wants everything for me. I give all to him because through him all things come.

God Bless Their Souls!

(Dedicated to Georgeann White)

God bless their souls
When they talk behind your back
God bless their souls
When jealousy guides them
God bless their souls
When righteous people hurt you
God bless their souls
When they misinterpret your happiness
God bless their souls
And bring them
Into the light!

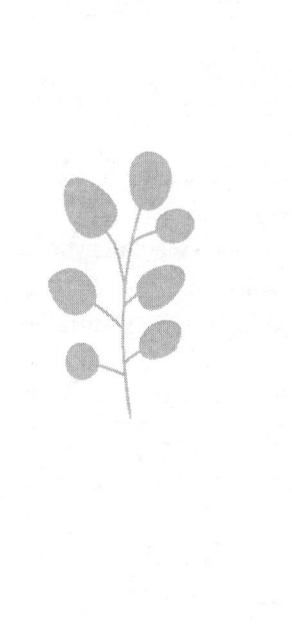

God Reveals Truths

God reveals the truth
Inside our lives
He reveals the
Pretending
He reveals the
Masks
He reveals the
Egos
He reveals the
Spiritual light
He ignites it
He lets it shine bright
So that others can see
He shines a brilliant light through us
So others will follow Him

Poems *of* Courage

This collection of poems is about overcoming fears, learning to protect my heart and standing strong when others try to manipulate you. I wrote the poem *Justice* as a response to manipulation and corruption around me at work and in my personal life. Sometimes, because you are a nice person, others take advantage of you, make such a mess of things, and walk away. No matter what others say or think, God knows my heart, he knows the truth, and he is the only judge.

I wrote *Quietly* about a woman at my church who never complains and is always caught caring for or serving others. Yet, in her own life she has a daughter who is waiting for a kidney transplant and other personal struggles. I wanted her to know that she is not alone, that God is right there with her, and he notices everything.

I wrote *God Picked You* to the man who was in charge of organizing all the work on our mission trip to Lakeshore, Mississippi. On one of our last days people were taking all of their complaints to him. He was pretty frustrated and not sure he would be a leader on a trip like this again. This poem is about the courage it takes to be a leader and about how God sees in us what we may not see in ourselves.

Justice

I shall remain silent
For it is the Lord
Who leads the way
I shall remain silent
As He dissolves differences
And changes perceptions
I shall remain silent
And let the Lord justify me
He is my defender
He is my armor and shield
I shall remain silent
And watch in awe
At His wondrous works
For He is my only judge
Justice

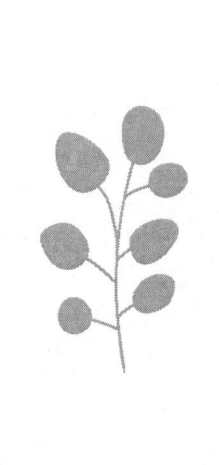

Fear

Fear makes me
Frozen in time
Fear hurts my family
Fear harms my future
Fear is not of God
Through Jesus I overcome
My fear
I will fight fear
With love
I will overcome fear
With faith
Not my will…
But your will be done
Jesus
Through you……love,
happiness, and
great joy!

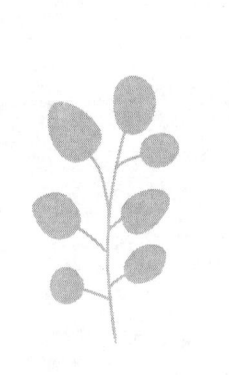

Standing Strong

Today I am standing strong
In the Light
In His Grace
I am standing strong
He wants me to
Walk in faith
Because it gives me strength
God helped me to stand strong
Because I am His beautiful child
Stand up for God
Stand strong
Stand in hope
Stand in faith
Stand in the light
Stand strong

God Picked You!

(Dedicated to Bob Bosquez)

There are many people
Who can lead
But God picked you
There are all kinds
Of critics in the world
But God picked you
Others have your
Decisive nature
But God picked you
There are many people
With visions and dreams
But God picked you
Others get the job done
With perseverance
But God picked you
There are different ways to lead
With Humility, strength and compassion
But God picked you
So when you ask yourself,
"Why me?"
Because, God picked you!

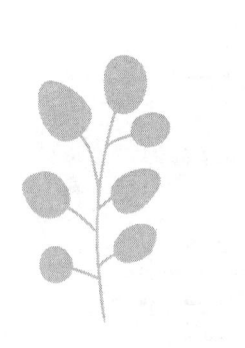

Quietly

(Dedicated to Janelle Pond)

Quietly you toil
Quietly you hug
Quietly through you
He sends gifts from above
Quietly you give
All your pain to Him
Quietly you rest
Your worries
Quietly you love
Quietly you strive
To understand His
Journey for you

Quietly you touch
Others' lives
Quietly you walk
Listening to others'
Strife
Quietly He blesses You
With endurance
Remain steadfast
He is watching over you
Quietly you touch many
Hearts
He notices everything!

Poems *of* Love

These poems are ones that touch my heart. They demonstrate God's unending love for us. He takes care of us, nurtures, and guides us. Even when we think that we are all alone, he is right there carrying us and teaching us.

The poem *Words of Gold* is written about my father. I was very close to my father. There were many times throughout my life that I wouldn't have to say anything, but my father knew I was troubled or hurting. I would never take my troubles to my mother, just my father. He would never judge or tell me what to do; he would only gently guide me. He told me to always remember this was my home and I was always welcome.

A Letter to Chris is a poem about my eldest brother who just when his adult life was starting he was diagnosed with cancer. After a five year struggle, he passed. We fought as kids and grew close as adults. I read the 23rd Psalm at his funeral, but I never told him I loved him, which is something I regretted after he passed.

After I was divorced and my children were out of a life of turmoil and into a stable, peaceful life, I wrote these poems to them. I never wanted them to be hurt or have to go through a divorce, but sometimes we don't get to control everything in our lives.

The poem *Perception* is a heart-wrenching poem that I wrote in one of my darkest hours. Sometimes we think we are making wise and honorable decisions in the midst of confusion, but our decisions are made on what we see in front of us. Sometimes what is in front of us is a lie, and we are the only ones who don't know it. It is our perception.

God's Tender Care is a poem I wrote about how loving and tender God is, how he has helped me see the truth from the lies, and how he has healed me and made me stronger.

A Love for a Daughter I wrote, with my own father in mind, to a man who helped me when others turned their backs out of fear. He told me that he cared about me and felt I was like a daughter to him.

Compassion I wrote to a friend about what it really means. This person's life seemed wonderful but lacked the depth that compassion brings in one's life. It is from deep within my heart and about how important it is sometimes to fight the fights that count.

Calm was written to describe a feeling I had rarely felt in the past 25 years. Oh my goodness, how serene it feels and how safe it feels. Calm is how I feel when God touches me and quiets my worries and fears.

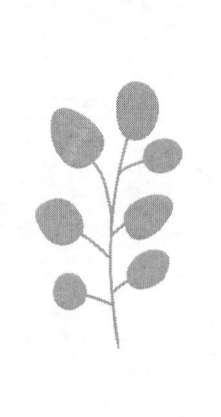

Compassion

A passionate devotion
To a person
Someone you would
Walk through fire for
A faithfulness
Beyond compare
There is no turning back!
Facing the storm
With all your being
An intimate relationship
Where hearts lock
And move forward
Together

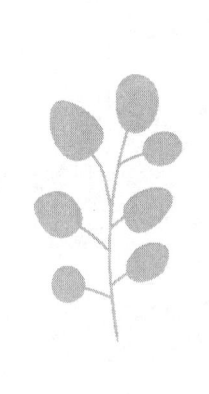

God Gifts Us

God gifts us
With his spirit
He gives us
All we need
Gifts of kindness
Gifts of peace
Gifts of love
We blossom and create
Our artistic talents emerge
Our inspiring happiness
And friendly nature
Flourish and become contagious
God gifts us
So we can spread His love
Throughout the world

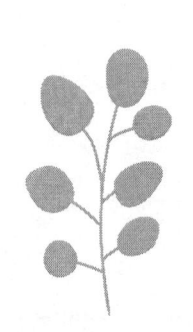

God Touched Me!

One night when all was lost
God touched me!
He took my hand
He lifted me up
He dried off my tears
He healed my heart
He carried me on a journey
He soothed my fears
He brought me to a new world
Of smiling faces
He reached deep in my soul
He showed me the beauty inside me
One night when all was lost
God touched me!

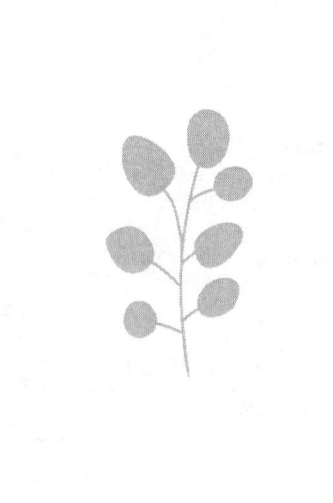

Calm

Serene inner peace
Silence is beautiful
The sun rising and
Casting a colorful display
Outside my window
As I open my eyes
To greet the day
I smile a sleepy smile
As God shines His
Light on me
His love and kindness
Bring me peace and calm
I walk peacefully
The country road before me
A gentle breeze blows
He caresses me and
Heals me inside and out
Hope and love replace
Fear and anxiety
I feel stronger and happier
Each day
As the sun goes down
Bright stars dance in the
Sky to keep me
In the light at night

God tucks me in with
A cuddly hug of
Serene silence and
Inner peace
His love endures all
As I fall gently off
To sleep
He gives me happy
Dreams
Of hopeful and happier
Tomorrows
I feel at home
With Him
Calm
Serene
Loved

Heaven Above

Heaven above
Looks down
On you, my child
Angels are guiding you
They stand watch
Protecting you
Heaven above
Loves you, my child
No more nightmares exist
For Heaven above
Sings out a
Chorus of love,
My child
Heaven above has
Guardian angels
Bringing you many gifts

An Abundance of
Joy, peace and love
Are coming your way
Accept these gifts
From God
With an open heart

For you are chosen
To fulfill
A special purpose
God has planned
His will be done

Words of Gold

(Dedicated to Clifford A. Husereau)

Thank you for being my friend
Keeping me safe and warm
Guiding me and caring about me
I never realized how much
I appreciated you
Relied on you
And deeply loved you
Someone I could tell anything to
Yet no judgment would you deliver
A gentle nudge in the right direction
I could count on you
Your words were like
Gold
I hope someday to meet a man
Whose words are like
Gold
Not like shifting sand
Words of Gold
Make me feel safe
And secure
They make me feel
Loved

Thank you for
Your words of Gold
Your loving nudges
Your gentle guidance
Your warm, everlasting hugs
I miss them

A Letter to Chris

(Dedicated to my brother, who died young)

Today I saw you
I had been longing to see you
For so long
It hurt to see you struggle
For so many years
Your body deteriorating
Your beautiful smile fading
And your hair disappearing
We grew so close to one another
After so many years of
Arguing and fighting
I could see your respect and
Admiration for me
As I became a young woman
We were so close at
The end
But I never got to tell you
How much I loved you
How much I admired you
What a beautiful inspiration you
Were at the end

I could see God's love in
Your face
After a dreary, overcast day
You passed
There was silence in the room
A sigh of relief that your struggles were over
Then I remember so clearly
The sun came out
There was a beautiful
Rainbow in the sky
God's promise of eternal life
Mark and I grew close
During those days
Now we look out for each other
We value our love for one another
A lesson you taught us
Through your struggles
You touched so many lives
God gave you love
To share with us
It has sustained us
All of these years
I love you
For you were a beautiful, brother

Jena

(Dedicated to my beautiful daughter)

Beautiful, delightful, lighthearted
You touch my heart
For you truly are
A gift from God
We worried and prayed for
Your safe and healthy arrival
God blessed us with your
Sunshine smile, your quick-witted humor
And your carefree, fun-loving laugh
You are a beauty to behold
In the morning when you can
Hardly open your eyes
And you are an angel in the darkness
When I hug you and
Tuck you in at night
God gave us a lovely, creative beauty
To behold
You touch lives with your
Innocent, giving heart

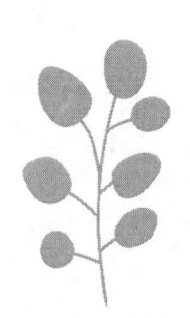

Jahvahka

(Dedicated to my handsome son)

Sometimes I look at you
And I see my brother, Chris
You are so smart
So tender and loving
I cherish that
You and I are so close
You are growing into a
Fine, young man
I can't get over how
Mature you are
Jahvahka, you are close
To my heart
For you were the first
You were planned
You were deeply loved
Ever changing as a baby
A surprise package
Beyond all of our expectations
Jahvahka, I love you
Each night as I tuck you in
I savor these moments
Pretty soon you will be a man
And you won't need me

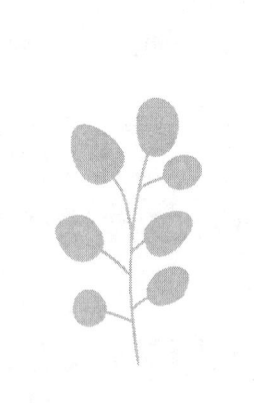

Essence

The Essence of
Love
Is our Savior
The Essence of
Our existence
Is one who had
A dream
Of great things!
Who walked through
The storms of life
On a journey
To the father
The Essence of
Love
Is walking hand in hand
With Jesus

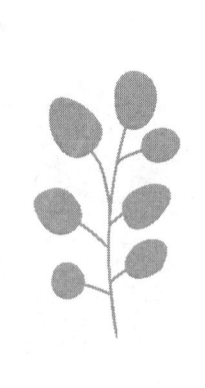

A Love for a Daughter

(Dedicated to Mr. Mac)

A love for a daughter
Is strong and everlasting
The security it renders
The warmth and trust it brings
Sustains her throughout her life
A resting place she can rely on
For comfort and endearing support
A love for a daughter
Is precious and fragile
It is guarded like a treasure chest

Someone you will protect
With all your being
A love for a daughter
Is deep with compassion
Because she is a part of you
A love for a daughter
Lives on past your
Years
Cherish your time
Together
Hold tight to your
Love
For a love for a daughter is …
Neverending!

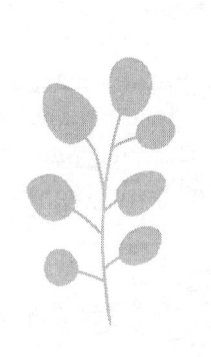

Perception

My perception waivers
From day to day
Sometimes I see
God's work in front
Of me so clearly…
It's breathtaking!
Other times I struggle
To see what He wants of me
I am fearful, doubtful,
And anxious
I toss and turn
I cry…
I call out His name
He comes to
Comfort and soothe me
He shows me the way
He tells me He hasn't
Left my side
I hang tight to
His hand
We walk together
He shows me
The wonders of His works
I am inspired
He lets go of my hand
For a short while

I feel my wings
Take flight
I am happy
There is no weight
Holding me down
I smile; I feel loved
I stop and turn towards Him
I put out my hand
He takes it
We walk together in
Silence, peace, and serenity
I know I am His child
He cares and loves me
He is showing me
A new life…
A new way…
I trust only in Him
For His love transcends
All earthly perceptions
I have a new perception
Of my life…
I am loved eternally
He has touched me!

God's Tender Care

I am under God's tender care
His gentle hand guides me
Down a winding path
He seems to know the way
But I cannot see where
He is leading me
I am calm and content
For I trust only in Him
My heart is peaceful
The way is easy
I am under God's tender care
His grace and mercy
Give me faith and hope
I am under God's tender care
I am comfortable in the silence
He wraps me in His Love
I am under God's tender care
Nothing can hurt me here
For He protects me
I am under God's tender care
I walk in the light
My spirit soars
My wings take flight
I am under God's tender care

Poems *of* Eternal Life

These poems were written about death and how God showed me that it is not final and it is no more. There is only eternal life. This was important for me to help my children through the grieving process of their father's death. I wrote *Laid to Rest* about the death of my children's father.

Celebrate Life I wrote to comfort a friend and his family during a time when their father was dying of a terminal illness. We spent many hours talking about his father and from our conversations I wrote this poem. Like many of the poems I have written for others, this one helped me change my perception about death.

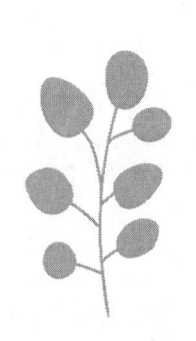

Laid to Rest

(Dedicated to Johnnathon Blaylock)

All your worries
Are now laid to rest
Your fears and pain
Have subsided
Accounts, weights, and measures
Are now dissolved
Dark memories
Are laid to rest
Confusion and distortions
Are clear
The answers revealed
You are laid to rest

In the comfort of
God's Grace and Mercy
Be at peace
Smile on your loved ones
Enjoy the serene surroundings
Of your new home
In Heaven
You are laid to rest
Your memory lives on
In those whose lives
You touched
You are laid to rest

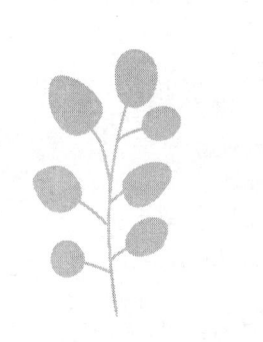

Celebrate Life

(Dedicated to the family of Crawford Hill)

When you think of your loved one…
The loss that you feel…stop and celebrate a beautiful life
Have a party inside your heart
Put a smile on your face… celebrate a beautiful life
That has touched your heart, molded your future,
Expressed their love…in all of the things
That reminds you of them,
So when you're sad…
And a tear
Trickles down your face
STOP!
Celebrate a beautiful life
Have a party inside
Your heart
Put a smile on your face
Because someone has
Just reached out and touched you
From heaven!

Poems of Grace

God's grace is so beautiful. To understand that it is given and not earned is something huge that many people struggle to understand. I wrote *Grace* to describe this.

During and after the death of my children's father, I felt God's loving hand taking care of me. Every time I worried about the future, he brought an answer. When I finally realized I don't need to worry anymore, I wrote *God is Taking Care of Me*.

One day in church a former pastor from another church spoke about God's dream for us. In the middle of this, God gave me this poem. It gave me hope that God is guiding me to a new life full of happiness and love. I wrote *God has a Dream* and dedicated it to that pastor. My hope is that he will read it for the first time in my published book.

Finally, I wrote *Peace*. I have peace in my life, because I turned to God to get me through my darkest hour and guide me to walk closer to him. I have peace and it feels "free" and "calm." I do not worry about the future, because it is in God's tender-loving hands. I want my children to know God is who gets you through the good times and the bad times.

God is Taking Care of Me

I can't explain it
But I can see God's hand at work
Like I've never seen it before
God is taking care of me
He loves me so much
It is unexplainable
His immense love for me
He nurtures and guides me
God is taking care of me
He provides everything I need
I don't worry anymore
God is taking care of me
He has shown me a
Beautiful promise
Beyond my dreams

I am a witness of
His great power and spirit
God is taking care of me
I am blessed by His
Grace and mercy
I have a loving father
Who knew me before
I was formed in the womb
He will never leave me
God is taking care of me

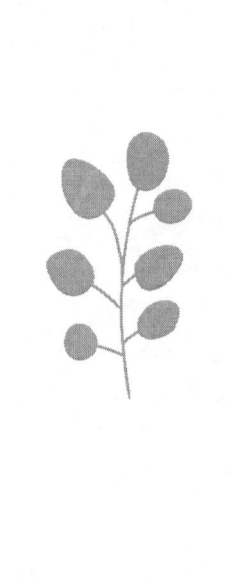

God Has a Dream

(Dedicated to Dwight Murphy)

God has a dream
For you and me
Throughout our lifetime
He takes us on a journey
To that dream
We are His beautiful children
His great work of art
God has a dream
He is always standing near
Walking with you
To that place
Deep within your heart
Where He resides

He has laid out a
Canvas of your Life
He paints it in your dreams
For you to follow
God has a dream
To take you high
Up in the mountains

To look out in awe at his wondrous works
And across the vast seas
At how deep and infinite his love is
God has a dream
Your life can unfold
Through Him
Give all to Him
For God has a dream
That will
Never fail

Grace

A gift from God
So beautiful
Exceeding all expectations
A gentle kindness
Bestowed upon us
A recognition
Of what we are
Truly meant to be
Created in His Image
Our souls soar
In His light
He guides us home
To His warmth
And Love

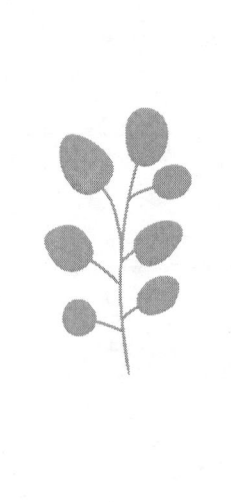

Peace

A serene feeling of
Calm and quiet
The gentle touch of
His hand quieting
My heart
Healing my soul
With His love
And tender guidance
Peace
An extraordinary
Leap of faith
To surrender everything
To God
Peace